CA
BRIN
GOVERNMENTS?

MEMES, DESIGN AND POLITICS

METAHAVEN

CONTENTS

We have all seen how an appropriate and well-timed joke can sometimes influence even grim tyrants... The most violent tyrants put up with their clowns and fools, though these often made them the butt of open insults.
Desiderius Erasmus, *The Praise of Folly*, 1509.

A bottle of pop, a big banana
We're from southern Louisiana
That's a lie, that's a fib
We're from Colorado
From: C.H. Ainsworth, "Jump Rope Verses around the United States," *Western Folklore* 20, 1961, 121. Cited in Susan Stewart, *Nonsense*.

A Definition of Now, Metahaven 2012.

INTRODUCTION

MAY, 2012

I'm sifting through a bunch of old records, and the smell of dusty cardboard and vinyl, softened by the summer heat, fills the decrepit record store. Passing through the same old Michael Boltons and Ultravoxes, I pause at an album by George Clinton, the legendary founder of Funkadelic. The album title is Some of My Best Jokes Are Friends. *It was released in 1985.*

A few hours later, I'm browsing the internet looking for evidence of political reform in Europe after the financial crisis. There is almost nothing; it's the same old system obsessively staring at its own growth, or the lack thereof. Except for Iceland. Its constitution was rewritten by "crowdsourcing"—a trendy word for getting direct input from as many people as possible. The country brings its own corrupted bankers to court, where it has some trouble getting them convicted.[1] The mayor of Reykjavík, Jón Gnarr Kristinsson, is a comedian; his party, the Best Party, became popular by parodying ruling politicians. In a pleasant combination of dispassionate rationality and raving madness, Iceland—a state with the population of a small city—seems a laboratory for reinventing politics. In Italy, a new kind of populist movement is gaining ground, headed by the comedian Beppe Grillo. His slogan Vaffanculo *("Fuck off") has hundreds of thousands in its grip; his performances are entertaining political rants that promote self-organization and human values. Grillo is against Italy's participation in the euro currency and, by virtue of that position only, fits into Europe's centrist-totalitarian media discourse as a "dangerous" politician. His weapon is comedy, and what makes it effective is its natural juxtaposition to* both *the pompous "common sense" of technocratic bailout rule* and *the perverted, corrupted olicharchy of Berlusconi. Yes, Grillo is a merciless populist; but that's not why he is popular.*

On Twitter, I find an essay by the Deterritorial Support Group (DSG), a think tank band of London-based graphic activists. Goatse As Industrial Sabotage *links perverse internet images to political graphic design from the 1970s. DSG's thesis is as strangely plausible as it is, in a political sense, hilarious.*

A friend reminds me of Ethan Zuckerman's Cute Cat Theory of Digital Activism. *It holds that a digital platform where many people exchange pictures of cute cats is also an excellent place for political activism: if the state were to shut it down, people would protest because they could no longer exchange pictures of cute cats. (More likely, if this did happen, they would find* another *platform* to *exchange pictures of cute cats). Zuckerman contends that it is inherently fruitful to embed messages of political activism within widely popular online platforms, so that subversive content can't be easily isolated by authoritarians.*

A question shapes itself in the early morning hours. Is it possible that graphic design has only one thing left to do, which is posting itself on the internet? And—to go a little bit further—is it possible that jokes have an untapped political power, which was historically always present but never so useful and necessary as now? Could, then, the leftovers of graphic design be turned into jokes? Might—through this re-allegiance—design rediscover actual societal impact? *Can jokes scale? Can they* supersize? *Can we laugh so loudly at those in power that they fall? Can jokes, in fact, bring down governments?*

NOVEMBER, 2012

We are told this is a time for tough decisions and certainly not a time for jokes. Governments of liberals, centre-right conservatives and social democrats have declared austerity throughout Europe. Their policies are a cocktail of the once-opposed extremes of their respective ideologies: there will be reduced public services (hail neoliberals), and there will, at the same time, be higher taxes (hail social democrats). Injustice is now *fair.*

Austerity is promoted and imposed by a techno-financial superclass of managers. The austerity elite does not live in the countries where its regimes are imposed, and it most certainly does not live in the social circles affected by it. Where its rule is the harshest this superclass goes by the name of the *troika*. Comprised of the International Monetary Fund (IMF), European Central Bank (ECB) and European Commission (EC), this roaming triumvirate of experts specialises in summary judgments of EU countries.

Austerity is *potentially unlimited*. It has *no boundaries*. No austerity elite is willing to say: until here, and no further. The humanitarian crisis of austerity is none of its business.

In unleashing austerity on its constituents, the political superclass has opened up a Pandora's box of disastrous consequences. It has awakened and emboldened powerful enemies. Not just of austerity, but of democracy itself.

Politicians in Europe are more afraid of financial markets than of their own people. Financial markets exercise a form of "direct democracy" over our lives everyday via the stock exchange, the bond markets, the ratings agencies, the banks, financial service providers and their products. While people may have their say every four to five years in parliamentary elections, they produce—at best—*parodies* of regime change. When financial trader Alessio Rastani, in a BBC interview, famously asserted that "governments don't run the world, Goldman Sachs does" it left the presenters in a real state of shock. Did it really? The BBC journalists were actually surprised that it is profitable to cripple countries, as Rastani assured them was the case. Indeed, as of July 2012, no less than five key European financial executives are former employees of Goldman Sachs: Peter Sutherland, the Irish Director-General of the World Trade Organization; Italian prime minister Mario Monti; Greek prime minister Lucas Papademos; Petros Christodoulou, who leads Greece's national debt management agency[2], and Mario Draghi, the Italian President of the ECB. On November 26, 2012, Mark Carney was named head of the Bank of England. He also previously worked at Goldman Sachs.[3]

In 2009 British author Mark Fisher coined the term "capitalist realism" to describe this paradigm of government. In a (still) notionally democratic system a state of permanent crisis, either looming or actual, is normalized. Capitalism is then established as "the only viable political and economic system" to the extent that "it is now impossible even to *imagine* a coherent alternative to it."[4] Fisher's American counterpart, the anthropologist David Graeber, located the key financial-political problem in the phenomenon of debt. In his book *Debt: The First 5,000 Years*, Graeber observed that "the last thirty years have seen the construction of a vast bureaucratic apparatus for the creation and maintenance of hopelessness, a giant machine designed, first and foremost, to destroy any sense of possible alternative futures [...]" so that "those who challenge existing power arrangements can never, under any circumstances, be perceived to win."[5] This analysis is right on the money, literally. The political system, practice and governing ideology of capitalist realism functions as a frameset which forces its political opponents to "speak the same language." By means of such a "discourse"—an interplaying set of words, meanings, symbols and implications (a system, indeed, of "making sense" of the world)—any alternative (by the oppressed) must first be rendered in the language and protocol of the oppressor.

There is, at first sight, nothing too funny about the death of social democracy. "Luxury for everyone" is now "financial oligarchy against the masses". Pretty much everyone except the occasional oligarch's beautiful daughter is doing worse than their parents did, in terms of job prospects and job security, whereas social development is stifled by an over-regulated and monetised public sphere. In the Netherlands, for example, alongside grave austerity, and despite millions of square meters of vacant office space being available as part of this country's real estate bubble, squatting has been declared a criminal offense. Countries the West looks up to for their economic growth, such as Brazil, Russia, India and China, invariably show much steeper rich–poor divides than any

INTRODUCTION

Western government of the past 20 years would have deemed acceptable. It is a statement of fact that we have entered a world of drastic inequality—its political compass pointed toward much more of it. Graeber's "99%" vs. "1%" binary became one of the Occupy movement's dominant motifs—exposing how fundamental social inequality has become to Western governance. Worse, this ideology of resource distribution cannot be expelled from there by the conventional political and media channels.

Designers are, on the whole, to be found on the poorer side of that watershed. We've been told, by the likes of Richard Florida, that our proficiency at brewing lattes and baking cupcakes, our aptness at drinking and eating them clad in angular hipsterwear, while posting pictures of ourselves and all of our food on Tumblr, constitutes a self-propelling socio-economic *Wunderbaum* called "creativity." Richard Florida's wealth cloud of gallery openings, furniture stores and coffee and wine bars is some sort of 72 dpi parody of the 19th century bourgeoisie's transformation of the inner city into a theme park for the *flâneur*. Indeed, the decorative paintings of our erstwhile *salons* have become digital files on laptop screens, in dilapidated, sub-subrented, barely inhabitable apartments. There must, however, be many ways in which the labour of designers can be politicised in the age of capitalist realism. How can graphic designers, for example, deploy their labour against the austerity elites? Depicted as the solemn care-takers of a hatchet job that just must be done, the austerity elites and their capitalist realist hordes get away with it—supposedly to bring economies back into a healthy shape, "paying back" fictional billions of toxic assets and nonexistent resourc-es, by slashing the state while raising taxes. Not only are the cutbacks hammering fragile human ecosystems into poverty at the pleasure of banks and speculators, as is happening in Greece, Italy, Portugal and Spain; for some, the job of cutting and slashing the public sector is an activity at the very heart of their political beliefs. What gets presented as a "natural" program to re-establish a "balanced budget" is in fact a vehicle to achieve a particular, and emphatically political, outcome.

The bankruptcy of conventional tactics at maintaining any believable "opposition" against this political state of emergency reveals itself ev-erywhere. Usually, a principled announcement of resistance against any unfairness (the slashing of benefits, pensions, child care, healthcare, etc.) lands centre-left political parties some electoral gains. When elections are over, compliance begins; a lust for power (er, "responsibility," sorry) brings about a forced marriage with what nominally counts as that party's strong political opponent, usually a pro-austerity centre-right party which has itself maintained power by modeling its politics along the lines of the extreme right. Austerity is instituted as expected, and the "explaining" of its technocratic programming language may begin. The rule of austerity, therefore, is closely tied to the older idea of a "Third Way," where a rational consensus between opposed political agents led to a package deal going beyond any notion of conflict or opposition.[6]

The politics of capitalist realism can only be countered by a strategy which removes itself from its political-discursive frame. Instead of being heard and listened to, people are continuously being told they have no idea of the magnitude of the threat that is underway—which is a manner of silencing them and enforcing a frame of reference.

If your country is not already like Greece, it will require lots of austerity to not become like Greece. If your country is already like Greece, or worse, it will need an even larger austerity package to "improve its economic outlook." What is needed is a political intervention that removes itself from the frame of this ongoing political and social state of emergency.

So, how might graphic designers contribute? The failure of corrupted political entities to properly represent *anyone* who mandated them to assume governing power is somewhat analogous to the crisis confronted by graphic designers in their eroding role as mediators and representatives of institutions. We might begin to understand the reign of austerity from a different angle if we take into consideration how graphic design's social role has changed with it. Design, gradually but certainly, has shifted from being a middleman in the social fabric between people and institutions, to functioning as a direct *index* of conditions of life and work in a given place. In other words, design is a direct agent of the socio-political realities lived by its makers. To a large extent, this is due to the fact that many graphic designers are short on, or out of, work. The institutions they were educated and trained to serve have either ceased to exist, or no longer commission them in the ways they once did. Designers used to be everything between enlightened technicians-craftsmen, cynical enablers of the predictable, principled technocrats, or impassioned fighters for a better world. In all these roles, they were also *gatekeepers*. The world as it gets mediated through information from "senders" to "receivers" passed through the designer's hands, and often through a printing press. The designer once operated at the behest of an institution, be it the Postal Service, or a museum, or the subway, which maintained the infrastructure of social democracy. Now that this infrastructure has collapsed, designers are becoming increasingly unpaid, and are also "released" from the frame that gave their activity meaning and purpose within the socio-democratic fabric. This relative loss makes designers both qualified, and ready, to take the next step.

DISRUPTION

In *Capitalist Realism*, Fisher offers a hopeful note. He predicts that a politics of fear enslaved by capital is vulnerable to even the slightest of ripples across its surface. Precisely because the system is made and maintained by technocratic control freaks, it is easily disrupted. Fisher says, "the long, dark night of the end of history has to be grasped as an enormous opportunity. The very oppressive pervasiveness of capitalist realism means that even glimmers of alternative political and economic possibilities can have a disproportionately great effect. The tiniest event can tear a hole in the grey curtain of reaction which has marked the horizons of possibility under capitalist realism. From a situation in which nothing can happen, suddenly anything is possible again."[7]

This essay is concerned with the disruption Fisher hints at in the closing remarks of *Capitalist Realism*. We will look for glimmers of such alternative realities, drawing on the resources of a graphic design dismissed from its former duties. The joke has the capacity to resist and overturn the frame of reference imposed by any political status quo—including that of capitalist realism. The joke has an untapped power to disrupt—a power far greater than we thought. On the internet, jokes may "scale" quickly and reach hundreds, thousands, tens of thousands, hundreds of thousands, millions of people in the course of a few minutes, if they are contagious enough to catch on.

Fisher's assumptions about the susceptibility of capitalist realism to disruption have so far proven correct. 2010 and 2011 were years of uprising, with protests, even revolutions, occurring throughout North Africa, the United States and Europe. The disclosures of WikiLeaks, popular revolutions in the Arab world against western-backed dictators, Occupy Wall Street's civic invasion of the joint arena of finance capital and the state, and Anonymous's defacements of and denial-of-service attacks against the superstructure of corporations and governments, are an expression not just of anger but also of new forms of collectivism and political organization. The struggles took to the streets and swept the internet—meaning, effectively, the re-politicisation of an entire generation of youth raised under capitalist realism. As a result, the London headquarters of the Conservative Party were in 2010's "Winter of Protest" suddenly besieged by "girls dressed like Lady Gaga" and "boys wearing pixie boots and ironic medallions".[8]

The mobilisations set off from a grid of mobile internet and online social media, smartphones, and digital cameras. This is a pattern common to all contemporary protests: the tools are means of coordination, sharing and mass communication all at the same time. That is, a group can coordinate amongst itself so it knows its own moves. New information can influence decision-making instantly, unfiltered by any central apparatus. These same tools are not just as a movement's field radio, but also its mass media broadcasting instruments. Facebook and Twitter replaced hierarchy and bureaucracy; smartphone in hand, coordination now came for free. And along with its tools, the network injected its own indigenous culture into protest. Rather than relying on the classical graphic design strategies developed for political protest, the network has been breeding a native approach to protest in which the anonymity or pseudonimity of the sender provided a break with the institutional mode of communication, from a known "sender" to an unknown "receiver," engrained even in graphic design's most idealist models of practice. Anonymity *also* breaks with a culture of online "real name accountability" promoted by both some of the world's major social networking sites, as well as internet regulators.

One of the most pervasive network-native approaches to protest was formed in the unlikely environs of an online message board called 4chan.org. 4chan is an image forum that rose to prominence and visibility in the mid-2000s, when a generation of net-native, bored trolls began to use it as a context to misbehave—originally united by an interest in Japanese-style manga and anime. The default moniker on 4chan to post stuff is *anonymous*—and, indeed, the notion of anonymity was

CAN JOKES BRING DOWN GOVERNMENTS?

central to the site from the start. The anonymity was inspired by similar Japanese image boards, where such anonymity constitutes a crucial human condition. And from 4chan's default user moniker sprang the notion of a collective called Anonymous, as is still spelled out by the site's FAQ page:

> "Anonymous" is the name assigned to a poster who does not enter text in to the [Name] field. Anonymous is not a single person, but rather, represents the collective whole of 4chan. He is a god amongst men. Anonymous invented the moon, assassinated former President David Palmer, and is also harder than the hardest metal known to man: diamond. His power level is rumored to be over nine thousand. He currently resides with his auntie and uncle in a town called Bel-Air (however, he is West Philadelphia born and raised). He does not forgive.[9]

Anonymous' activities as a "collective" began with their trolling of the Church of Scientology. In early 2008, a leaked video appeared on the web site Gawker.com consisting of a scary, incoherent motivational speech/performance by Scientology's most prominent member, Tom Cruise. Scientology had been trying to prevent the release of Cruise's speech at all costs and had had it taken down from YouTube before. The idea to then "raid", to "hack" or "take down" the Scientology website emerged on one of 4chan's discussion boards, and that's what subsequently happened. A notoriously humourless organisation, Scientology seemed to the emergent Anonymous to embody a sense of wrong, secrecy, and at the same time, camp. The protest ranged from denial-of-service attacks and exploiting Scientology's database, to physical demonstrations at Scientology branches in the US. An email sent to Gawker, announcing a protest at the Church of Scientology in Harlem, had the following tagline:

> We are Anonymous
> We are Legion
> We do not forgive
> We do not forget
> Expect us. [10]

Anonymous went from the online world of 4chan to a significant presence in physical space, and this back and forth continued right into the cyber-insurgency's 2011 engagement with Occupy Wall Street. But this transition did not bind or conform the group to the conventional logistics, aesthetics and rules of physical-space political protest. It emphatically developed new rules, strongly inspired by online anonymity. This included a white mask — loosely based on the British revolutionary Guy Fawkes — originally worn by the protagonist of Alan Moore's 1982 comic book *V for Vendetta*. The mask was hugely popularised by a 2006 film adaptation, and become so associated with protest that in February 2013 it was banned in repressive Gulf state Bahrain.Gabriella Coleman, an Associate Professor of Media Studies at New York University, notes that Anonymous "has become a political gateway for geeks (and others) to take action. Among other opportunities, Anonymous provides discrete micro-protest possibilities that aren't otherwise present, in a way that allows individuals to be part of something greater. [...] The decision to engage in political action has to happen somehow, via a concrete path of action, a set of events, or influences; Anonymous is precisely that path for many."[11] Anonymous as a "gateway," as a focal point or gathering strategy for activities that exceed the individual scope and scale, is a manner of describing its significance as a form of organising-without-organisation.

Anonymous and 4chan have been the *de facto* breeding estates for much of what we today see as network-native forms of protest. Those forms only became apparent quite recently, and they are hardly permanent. We might see Anonymous as an *open-ended in-group* — consisting of a potentially large number of individuals whose form of (dis)organisation is not based on any actively shared location or identity, other than their use of a computer, use of an internet chat room, and basic understanding of the English language. In this, Anonymous differs sharply from equally relevant, yet less scalable pseudonymous groups like The Invisible Committee. The Invisible Committee is a French anarchist collective which first published its pamphlet, *The Coming Insurrection*, in 2007.[12] This publication became "the principle piece of evidence in an anti-terrorism case in France directed against nine individuals who were arrested on November 11, 2008, mostly in the village of Tarnac. They were accused of 'criminal association for the purposes of terrorist activity' on the grounds that they were to have participated in the sabotage of overhead electrical lines on France's national railways. Although only scant circumstantial evidence has been presented against the nine, the French Interior Minister has publically associated them with the emergent threat of an 'ultra-left' movement, taking care to single out this book, described as a 'manual for terrorism,' which they are accused of authoring."[13]

The pamphlet premiered in the US in 2009 at an unscheduled event at a Barnes & Noble branch at Union Square in New York. A security guard tried to eject the crowd, without success; the crowd was then removed by the NYPD, and announced it

would move into Union Square park. After it left
Barnes & Noble,

> instead of proceeding directly to the park,
> the crowd moved next door to high-brand
> make-up outlet Sephora, where they were
> able to use their bodies to keep security
> away while the book was passed around for
> anyone to read aloud, others helping them-
> selves to free samples of bronzer and eyelin-
> er. After a few minutes the employees' pleas
> for the mob to leave were honoured as we
> took to the streets again, this time walking
> towards the nearest Starbucks—already on
> the alert for rowdy interventionist protests
> due to its long-running suppression of
> IWW union activity there. Cops arrived
> almost immediately; one person received a
> summons for disorderly conduct for reading
> atop a table. The group, which had dwindled
> after the appearance of about a dozen
> police, resigned themselves to reading,
> talking, and taunting the police from the
> park as they had previously decided.[14]

Just as Occupy reclaimed the public-corporate
space of Zucotti Park as "public" the 2009 readers
of *The Coming Insurrection* did so with Barnes &
Noble and Starbucks. The Invisible Committee,

Anonymous and Occupy Wall Street share similarities in content, and differences in form. *The Coming Insurrection* offered no easy targets, such as Scientology or PayPal, and no tools to pursue them. But its take on life under capitalist realist hopelessness is similar to that of Occupy and Anonymous. As the Committee wrote:

> No need to dwell too long on the three types of workers' sabotage: reducing the speed of work [...]; breaking the machines, or hindering their function; and divulging company secrets. Broadened to the dimension of the whole social factory, the principles of sabotage can be applied to both production and circulation. The technical infrastructure of the metropolis is vulnerable. Its flows amount to more than the transportation of people and commodities. [...] Nowadays sabotaging the social machine with any real effects involves reappropriating and reinventing the ways of interrupting its networks.[15]

Political action in the 21st century has moved beyond the manifesto. To achieve scale, it is deploying new strategies with viral properties and Darwinian survival skills.

THE MEME

THE MEME

The notion of the "meme" was introduced by the evolutionary biologist Richard Dawkins in the late 1970s as a way to describe what he called a "cultural gene." Memes are units of culture and behaviour which survive and spread via imitation and adaptation. Examples of memes are dances, catchphrases, greetings, hairstyles. On the internet, they can be pictures of cute cats, images of unicorns, they can be Rick Astley videos, or perverse sexual images. Memes play a distinct role in protest; they seem to be to the resistance of today, just as "political posters" were yesterday — the embodiment of shared ideas in a community. They can be JPEGs, or rumours. Indeed, part of their appeal is that memes seem to spread spontaneously. Paul Mason, the BBC's traveling chronicler of all things crisis-related, found that "with the internet [...] and above all with the advent of social media, it's become possible to observe the development of memes at an accelerated pace [...]. What happens is that ideas arise, are immediately 'market tested', and then are seen to either take off, bubble under, insinuate themselves into the mainstream, or, if they are deemed no good, disappear."[16] Mason contends that "[for] activists, memes create a kind of rough alternative to representative democracy." But he seems unsure as to their potential for permanence; are they anything more than "small cultural portions of the zeitgeist"?[17]

CAN JOKES BRING DOWN GOVERNMENTS?

Richard Dawkins was looking for a model that would explain how culture spreads and disseminates among people. In doing so, he applied Darwinistic principles to phenomena of human creation and imitation. "Cultural transmission," Dawkins said, "is analogous to genetic transmission in that, although basically conservative, it can give rise to a form of evolution." Genes are replicators. What is their cultural equivalent? The unit of transmission or imitation proposed by Dawkins has itself proven memetic; it is a ruthlessly pervasive idea that applies to phenomena we see all around us. He explained the name:

> 'Mimeme' comes from a suitable Greek root, but I want a monosyllable that sounds a bit like 'gene'. I hope my classicist friends will forgive me if I abbreviate mimeme to meme. If it is any consolation, it could alternatively be thought of as being related to 'memory', or to the French word même. It should be pronounced to rhyme with 'cream.'[18]

There are three qualities which define the success of memes: longevity, fecundity, and copying-fidelity. *Longevity* indicates how long a meme can last. *Fecundity* applies to the *appeal* of a meme, whether it is *catchy* and thus likely to spread. *Copying-fidelity* is about the strength of a meme to withstand mutation in the process of copying and imitation. It determines how much of the original core remains intact when the meme is in transmission. All three criteria also apply to jokes, but the joke was not mentioned by Dawkins as an example of a meme.

Some suggestions in this direction were made, however, by the cognitive scientist Douglas Hofstadter, a friend of Dawkins. Hofstadter was convinced that memes looked a lot like self-referential patterns, which would render them not only survival-minded and selfish—but also fundamentally absurd. An example of such self-referentiality is the Epimenides Paradox. The Cretan thinker Epimenides stated that "All Cretans are liars." The intricacies of this message, which says, "this statement is false," were explored by Hofstadter in his seminal book, *Gödel, Escher, Bach*.[19] Hofstadter brought memes to the attention of the readership of the *Scientific American* in the early 1980s, right before the idea caught on with the general public. Jeremy Trevelyan Burman reconstructs:

> In January of 1983, Hofstadter published an essay that directly discusses his interpretation of the memes proposal. This was inspired, he said, by letters from readers of his previous columns—in particular, by letters from Stephen Walton and Donald Going, who suggested that self-referential sentences

of the sort discussed in *Gödel, Escher, Bach* (e.g., 'This sentence is false') could be described as being afflicted by a kind of meaning-virus: self-reference parasitizes language, makes it inconsistent with itself, and then encourages the reader (as carrier) to

find or construct new instances of meaing-breaking self-reference.[20]

As Burman notes, "[both] Walton and Going were struck by the perniciousness of such sentences: the selfish way they invade a space of ideas and manage, merely by making copies of themselves all over the place, to take over a large portion of that space. Why do they not manage to overrun all of the space? It is a good question. The answer should be obvious to students of evolution: the sentences do not do so because of competition from other self-replicators."[21]

Memes are not phenomena *of* language; they are phenomena *with* language. From words which simply "annotate" a meme, conveying its minimally required meaning in a given context, to words which become an integral part of the meme's functioning. The standard internet meme is an image captioned with heavy type, superimposed on it "for humorous effect" (says Wikipedia). The sentences that are thus part of the image create some kind of strange loop or self-reference; but they also involve tacit knowledge on the part of the viewer. An example is the portrait of the Boromir character from the *Lord of the Rings* Trilogy, captioned with a sentence starting with "One does not simply..." In the original film, the actor Sean Bean says: "One does not simply walk into Mordor. Its black gates are guarded by more than just orks."[22] The "One does not simply..." meme has this sentence completed in different ways:

> One does not simply grow his dick six inches in three easy steps.
> One does not simply topple a Ugandan warlord by pressing "like" on Facebook.
> One does not simply log out of a friend's Facebook without making him gay.

A fictional, but widely known, point of reference is tinkered with to create new implications, to the point that one no longer thinks of Tolkien and Peter Jackson at all. But the remainder of that commonly held reference point, the tacit knowledge which is that I know that you know that I know that particular part of *The Lord of the Rings* enables the joke, *any joke*, that follows. If, for instance, the same sentence would be based on a film that no one has ever seen, its mention would never achieve the same immediate impact. A meme can tap into a collective memory and transform the "outcome" of a commonly held starting point to different ends.

Further study into the nature of self-referentiality was done by Susan Stewart in her legendary book, *Nonsense*. For Stewart, the category of "nonsense" is opposed to the category of "common sense making" through which what we think of as reality is established. By categorising something as "nonsense", "the legitimacy and rationality of sense making was left uncontaminated, unthreatened."[23]

It is not difficult to see a fundamental political procedure at work here. Isn't it exactly the day job of most politicians to *manage* reality and sense-making, deciding what *others* get to see as nonsense and what as legit? One is tempted to think here of Labour leader Ed Miliband's June, 2011 condemnation of nationwide strikes in the UK. In a BBC interview, Miliband gave the same answer to each different question posed to him by the journalist. "These strikes are wrong ... both sides should put aside the rhetoric and get around the negotiating table ..."[24] Time and again, Miliband hammered out the same words. His drone-like repetition of a single, studied phrase laid bare a structural protocol of governance, an inability to deviate from a script—even more preposterous when you think that Miliband is supposed to lead the opposition rather than govern the country. "Milibot," as the curious speech exercise became known, is an example of what Mark Fisher subsequently labeled "reality management."[25] It showed the impossibility of conducting "opposition" within the governing neoliberal frame, and the desperation of a politician trying to stan inside of it. Indeed, argued Stewart, "all discourse bears reference to a commonly held world. The discourse of common sense refers to the 'real world.' The discourse of nonsense refers to 'nothing.' In other words, it refers to itself, even though it must manufacture this 'nothing' out of a system of differences from the everyday world — the common stuff of social life — in order to be recognised as 'nothing.'"[26]

Nonsense also involves an element of "play." Boromir's "One does not simply…" bounces off from a widely known, and also slightly ridiculous phrase, and then goes on to take completely different directions with it. Stewart notes that

> Playing at fighting may be "not fighting," but it is not fighting on a different level of abstraction from other kinds of not fighting such as kissing, skipping rope, buying groceries, or singing "Happy Birthday." Play involves the manipulation of the conditions and contexts of messages and not simply a manipulation of the message itself. It is not, therefore, a shift within the domain of the everyday lifeworld: it is a shift to another domain of reality.[27]

CAN JOKES BRING DOWN GOVERNMENTS?

Memes take on a wide variety of forms and formats, but they do their work right in the human brain. Time, explained Dawkins, constitutes a major limit on the success of individual memes. No one person can do more than only a few things at once. Consequently, said Richard Dawkins, "if a meme is to dominate the attention of a human brain, it must do so at the expense of 'rival' memes."

Digital networks and social media do not dissolve the limits in attention that the human brain can give to any meme, but they do more or less solve two out of the three criteria that, according to Dawkins, determine a meme's success: longevity and copying-fidelity. Longevity of a meme in a digital network is in most cases guaranteed; a file may very well never be erased, and exist as long as the server exists that stores it. Then, copy-fidelity is guaranteed if a meme spreads by forwarding and reblogging a digital original. The meme's distribution into the gene pool is then completely without loss of quality. If a meme spreads by *imitation*, changes made in the process are still traceable when compared to an "original." Memes tend to be most successful if they get both copied *and* imitated.

When it comes to the meme's intrinsic fecundity digital networks don't give easy answers. Fecundity can't be presupposed just by something being on the internet. For every successful digital meme there are many thousands of failed attempts.

Many internet memes share distinctive features shaped by the unwritten rules of their commonly held world—be it software used, the online forum inhabited, a language spoken, or a set of aesthetic preferences. This, in turn, has led to the predictable misconception that anything produced following those unwritten rules is bound to become a meme. This is not the case. Successful memes balance their reference to a commonly held world with an element giving them a strikingly new meaning. The more "advanced" a meme is, the more its meaning will be implied by manipulation of the context in which the meme appears.

On November 18, 2011, Fred Baclagan, a retired FBI agent, sent an e-mail to his contact list:

> Hello all, I was very disturbed to find this in my inbox this morning: www.youtube.com/watch?v=oHg5SJYRHA0[28]

The link leads to the music video of Rick Astley's 1987 UK Charts, and Billboard Hot 100 No. 1 hit, *Never Gonna Give You Up*. The video is posted on YouTube under the title "RickRoll'd," and has been viewed 66,833,023 times, and counting. Baclagan's two Gmail accounts had been broken into by a hacktivist group called Antisec; his messages had been dumped online and Antisec made Baclagan aware of this fact by just sending him the

Rick Astley link. Such is the power of a successful meme's manipulation of context. In common parlance, being "Rickrolled" now means having been hacked and knowing it; Astley's song is a kiss of death. Baclagan was, in turn, inadvertently rickrolling his own contacts by just forwarding the Astley link. The origins of rickrolling lay in an amusing prankster meme on 4chan and other internet forums, where a seemingly promising, interesting and relevant link would lead an unsuspecting user to Rick Astley. It is a *gotcha* of sorts, which brings you "face-to-face with the ridiculous."[29]

Instead of merely entrapment in a false choice, the rickroll transports the user to what Susan Stewart called "another domain of reality." Instead of some parallel dream world, this is more of a conceptual overhaul in which all prior sense-making is erased, including the original meaning of Astley's own video.

Astley floats on an all-in, ready-to-roll commonly held world; like Boromir, there is tacit knowledge involved, of an audience's awareness of Rick Astley and his song. This is knowledge of the type "it's that guy/that song again" rather than "this is a young Rick Astley performing Stock Aitken and Waterman's 1987 monster hit."

But unlike the Boromir meme, the Astley video, as a meme, comes to imply a whole new set of things even *without* the superimposition of any new content.

The economist Thomas Schelling, in a 1958 experiment, famously found that when two people are to meet in New York City, but have not agreed on a place and time to do so (and have no way to coordinate their movements), they are likely to expect the other to show up at the clock in the middle of the Main Concourse of Grand Central Station at 12 noon. Schelling called such a space-time convergence a "focal point." Focal points arise not out of a prior agreement, but out of expectations. Memes can be focal points in man-made information space, in absence of a prior agreement. For example, the word "Tahrir Square" is a meme, a shorthand, for the entire Arab Spring. Many (in fact, too many) people who have never been to Tahrir Square refer to it with intimate familiarity, and expect others to understand what they mean when they utter the word "Tahrir." In London in 2011, "Tahrir Square" street signs began to appear; streets seemed, indeed, to become psychologically primed for revolt; its possibility was being introduced to areas where people might not have otherwise expected it. Tahrir in "memespace" converged with Tahrir in "meatspace"[30] as a self-evident focal point.

While Schelling laid bare the "prominence or conspicuousness" of focal points, later analysis compared focal points to conventions, or "common expectations or regularities."[31] It is a meme's ultimate reward to achieve the platinum status of "regularity";

but it is also the moment that its evolution has come to a halt. *Never Gonna Give You Up* has achieved such status; even retired FBI agents now get the in-joke. In an ecosystem of expectations, memes cash in on the primeval instincts which both sustain and continuously undercut the order of common sense that determines their place. Richard Dawkins claimed that a meme's dominance can only be curbed by rival memes. Any rival of a dominant meme must cash in on the same type of lowly desire which makes you devour tabloids and horoscopes; if one meme is low, its challenger must be lower, until the cycle is broken and a new one begins.

Some of these open secrets of fecundity have been probed by Bill Drummond and Jimmy Cauty, founders of the subversive British acid house group, The KLF. Their *Manual* to create UK No. 1 chart hits is extremely relevant to meme creation. In it, the duo sets out to amusingly prepare the reader to write, produce and release a UK Number One hit single. Drummond and Cauty develop a fairly comprehensive view on what it takes to reach a top position in the charts in the late 1980s. A *Smash Hits* music journalist named Neil Tennant had already laid some groundwork for this with his Pet Shop Boys seminal hit *West End Girls* — a UK and US Number One in 1985, its mood and lyrics alluding to, but not spelling out, class war in Britain.

Drummond and Cauty, in their song writing and production, promote a ruthless exploitation of the oasis of fecundity that is our gene pool. They reserve special praise for Stock, Aitken and Waterman—the latterday golden boys of the mixing room—who wrote and produced one hit after the other and dominated all the charts around the last half of the 1980s. Drummond and Cauty appear overjoyed at the inherent fecundity of Stock, Aitken and Waterman's production of monster hits. In particular, they admire *Never Gonna Give You Up* by Rick Astley. Right when Astley "hit the first line of the chorus on his debut single it was all over—the Number One position was guaranteed," write Drummond and Cauty:

> *"I'm never gonna give you up"*

It says it all. It's what every girl in the land whatever her age wants to hear her dream man tell her. Then to follow that line with:

> *"I'm never gonna let you down*
> *I'm never going to fool around or upset you."*

GENIUS.[32]

Stock, Aitken and Waterman produced not just songs but also entire acts. They "invented"

43

Bananarama, "created" Dead or Alive, "developed" Rick Astley, and "engineered" Kylie Minogue—each of them a platinum meme by itself. Stock, Aitken and Waterman's primary genius was, for the KLF, not so much in the overall stories their songs tell, but in the way catchy phrases are used. Stock, Aitken and Waterman are "able to spot a phrase [...] a line that the nation will know exactly what is being talked about, and then use it perfectly:

> "Fun Love and Money"
> "Showing Out"
> "Got To Be Certain"
> "Respectable"
> "Toy Boy"
> "Cross My Broken Heart"[33]

The three producers were themselves invisible, almost anonymous, behind the one-hit wonders they produced. They achieved their outcomes "masked" as Kylie Minogue or Rick Astley; looking like a baroque lollypop Marquis de Sade on one day (Dead or Alive), a proto-Rihanna R&B star (Princess—whose hit song is aptly called *Say I'm Your Number One*) on the next. Appearing as photo model secretaries (Mel & Kim), or pre-cybernetic, exploitative glam punks (Sigue Sigue Sputnik), each of Stock, Aitken and Waterman's avatars landed in the charts' top echelon out of nowhere, but always well below the bar of good taste. They changed the memetic landscape forever, and then disappeared.

Rival memes are rival dreams—the game is on not for a little bit of attention, or a little "like" here and there, but for a massive attack of the lowest common denominator, a rapture of the underbelly. Stock, Aitken and Waterman understood how such a project might be structured. While, indeed, internet memes use many elements floating in the common gene pool, these elements are almost always original acts by others; focal points and common references in a sea of information. Stock, Aitken and Waterman's "anonymity" behind the identities of their one-hit wonders was later eclipsed by the more overall facelessness of electronic dance music.

ENTER THE LOLCAT

Stock, Aitken and Waterman are the original "coders" of Rick Astley and thus, by proxy, of the "Rickroll." The trio is not known for its political activities, but that doesn't matter; the internet meme version of any piece of original work is not likely to sustain any of its intended values. The inherent ridiculousness of Boromir and Rick Astley qualifies an *indifference* to their original meaning, which is why the Rickroll meme is disruptive as a form while its "content" can consist of pure Stock, Aitken and Waterman.

CAN JOKES BRING DOWN GOVERNMENTS?

Many contemporary electronic images found on the internet are mere byproducts of the omnipresence of digital cameras. But they may lose that sense of innocence. A good example of an innocent image supercharged by the internet is the Lolcat. Lolcats are pictures of cats, superimposed with texts. Things are at their most hilarious when one tries to describe this type of image and its intended effect in a neutral manner; Wikipedia on February 21, 2013 found that a "lolcat (pronounced /ˈlɒlkæt/ lol-kat) is an image combining a photograph of a cat with text intended to contribute humour. [...] LOLcat is a composite of two words, 'lol' and 'cat'. 'LOL' stands for 'Laugh out Loud' or 'Laughing out Loud'; hence, lolcats are intended to be funny and to include jokes."[34] There is also something funny about seriously discussing "I can haz cheezburger", one of the best-known Lolcat memes. It is hard to discuss this trying to make sense. Cats are not eager to please; they are not likely to give in to any false choices presented to them. A Lolcat is the exact opposite of a Milibot; whereas Milibot desperately tries to force his puzzled listeners into "sense-making," Lolcat jumps out of the frame in which the false choice offered still seems to make any sense at all. Cats are today's political animals.

Every era, every generation, has to construct and reconstruct its political beliefs, and subsequent visuals, out of the stuff that surrounds it at any given moment. Protest signs will be made out of the cardboard, paper and textile available at that given time and place at a local hardware store; there is no hardware store selling "political" cardboard, so even at that material level, a transformation always has to be made. The same goes for the visual stuff of the internet; every generation will construct new, "political" beliefs out of it; out of all kinds of stuff which seemed initially non-political. This is especially striking when, in Europe, a not merely "non-political" but "post-political" generation grapples with its own politicisation under the aegis of austerity, neoliberalism, and financial-managerial-political corruption. For example, the cutting-edge Leftist political journal *Kittens,* published in London by The Wine and Cheese Appreciation Society of Greater London / Kittens Editorial Collective, features radical leftist writing *only* alongside photographs of cute kittens.[35] The strangest thing is that this combination further radicalises the message; *Kittens* acknowledges head-on the self-politicisation of an information space in which we were supposed to merely *enjoy ourselves.* In the absence of a "properly political" visual expression at hand, the stuff that is readily available, the internet's equivalent of cardboard, gets politicised just like Astley became the "Rickroll." In other words, every bit of visual information on the internet can, through the spectre of self-politicisation, become revolutionary, because it exists in a shared gene pool. Cats are especially useful and relevant. In *Wired* magazine, Gideon Lewis-Kraus has tracked the origins of the Lolcat back to Japan, where it is tied to a culture of online anonymity.[36] In a sense the Lolcat is to the average person what Sinitta was to Stock Aitken and Waterman. Lewis-Kraus traces why cats are so successful as internet symbols; he cites research about the relation between depression in humans and domestic cats. Indeed,

> your cat will like you best if you pretend that you don't desperately want to play with it all the time. ... The more neurotic the cat owner—the more desperate for fuzzy comfort and nuzzly security and uncondi-tional affection—the briefer the interactions that damn cat would allow.

And so,

> What we do on the internet is mostly "like" things, and while liking them we wait for our own content to be liked. We check our analytics as we await retweets. This is where the cats come in. A cat will not retrieve some dumb object so that you can throw it yet again ... That goes against everything cats stand for. Or more often sit. It's not just that

cats are unable to be anything but real; it's
that cats both know they are performing
and couldn't possibly care less about how
their performance is received ... What an
internet cat does is thus confront us with
how cravenly we ourselves court approval.
A cat, if it decides to love you, will do so only
on its own terms ... and the less you need
it, the better loved you are going to be.
The reason the lolcat says "oh hai" is because
he only *just noticed*, and certainly doesn't
care. ... He doesn't worry about you or
what you think. ... Thus is the internet cat
the realest cat of all.[37]

The Harvard University professor Ethan
Zuckerman has put forward what he calls a "Cute
Cat Theory of Digital Activism." Zuckerman proposed that with the user-generated content of the
"web 2.0," "we've embraced the idea that people are
going to share pictures of their cats, and now we build
sophisticated tools to make that easier to do. As a
result, we're creating a wealth of tech that's extremely
helpful for activists."[38] Zuckerman maintained that
the *network standard* built for sharing innocent cat
pictures has the resilience to then also carry the
exchanges of political activists. Memes prove that this
network standard can politicise the forms appearing
in it—from Rick Astley to the Lolcat.

CAN JOKES BRING DOWN GOVERNMENTS?

Memes on the internet descended from the in-jokes of the first, academic, users on the earliest bulletin boards. But in the mid-2000s, places like 4chan mass-produced and weaponised the online meme. They were vehicles of trolling and pranking to achieve the "lulz"—the open-ended making fun of the ridiculous. This is what drives 4chan, the anarchic culture around it and, to a certain extent, Anonymous. The internet, to 4chan, is a refuge from work, obligation, class, and name. It is a place where nothing really makes sense or is supposed to do so. Its single objective—the lulz—made 4chan into a pressure cooker for internet memes, and later, hacktivism. In a leaked 2011 threat assessment about the hacktivist network Anonymous, the US Department of Homeland Security National Cybersecurity and Communications Integration Center mentioned the meme, defining it as an "idea, behavior or style that spreads from person to person within a culture," whereas the lulz is "often used to denote laughter at someone who is a victim of a prank /malicious activity, or a reason for performing an action."[39]

Memes offer no explanation as to exactly why some of them work and others don't. They are hard to orchestrate at a larger scale; their success is always also an accident. Sheer quantity is about the only working strategy available. Memes can be compared to the evolution of the blues, and are perhaps a new "slave music" for the internet.

Drummond and Cauty in *The Manual* recall how every music is a reconfiguration of what came before and how "the complete history of the blues is based on a one chord structure, hundreds of thousands of songs using the same three basic chords in the same pattern. Through this seemingly rigid formula has come some of the twentieth century's greatest music."[40]

JOKES

Imagine a joke.

Imagine a joke that hits, again and again. A joke which self-replicates until it becomes the inescapable, omnipresent truth that hovers over each and every one of your political opponents.

Why jokes? And why now? Here's why. Jokes are low budget. They are among the cheapest goods we all have access to; they don't cost anything, and they work. They are austerity-proof. Jokes, like laughs, are contagious, even if their intention is deadly serious. Governments the world over are fortifying themselves against their own citizens, and most of all against their jokes. But jokes easily pass through the walls of the fortresses. *The joke is an open-source weapon of the public.*

Monty Python as early as 1969 fantasised about a joke so funny it could kill; whoever heard it or read it would die laughing. "Joke warfare" would be the military deployment of jokes by opposing armies.

The original maker of a joke often, and ideally, remains anonymous. He or she is truly a designer. We consider a designer here to be any formmaker, regardless of material; design is merely a few decisions on a form and its boundary—in jokes, this consists of what is said and importantly, what is not said. Jokes are mobile; a joke catching on means it is forwarded. With online social media and mobile internet, jokes are no longer dependent on purely oral transmission, television, or print and paper. Such is their longevity and copying-fidelity, that only the slightest remainder of a joke embedded in a new form can still carry the original.

Reality management, or sense-making, is establishing a frame in which certain things can be claimed not to have happened. Jokes are by virtue of their disruption of an existing order of "sense-making" very unwelcome guests in an age of austerity. We must cut spending now, there is no time to have arguments, these are serious times necessitating serious decisions, and so on—precisely the protocolar opiates emitted by every technocrat in power today which deny every alternative its right to sense-making, in the true spirit of capitalist realism. A governing class of bankers is extremely keen on being seen as simply those who know best—the smartest guys in the room, to quote the title of a documentary about Enron. The parliamentary alternatives to those bankers are always either fuming (racist) populists or powerless factions of the former Left, endlessly regrouping, and arguing internally. For the austerity elites this presents a terrific opportunity to get away with their own looming power vacuum.

Jokes can expose this vacuum. At the same time, there is a (growing) in-group that *gets the joke*. That in-group can equal almost the entire population of a country. In early 2011, Issandr el Amrani wrote about Hosni Mubarak — for decades, the butt of jokes when still president of Egypt:

> What would happen if you spent 30 years making fun of the same man? What if for the last decade, you had been mocking his imminent death — and yet he continued to stay alive, making all your jokes about his immortality seem a bit too uncomfortably close to the truth?

Indeed, as Egyptian actor Kamal al-Shinnawi adds, "The joke is the devastating weapon which the Egyptians used against the invaders and occupiers. It was the valiant guerrilla that penetrated the palaces of the rulers and the bastions of the tyrants, disrupting their repose and filling their heart with panic."[41] Jokes are an active, living and mobile form of disobedience. The Seriousness and Trustworthy Nature of Western Government has slowly but surely eroded the practice of the open ridicule of their power; we've simply unlearned it. Comedians — a few effective ones exempt –preside over their jokes like Steve Jobs used to over the Apple brand; such jokes remain the property of their maker wherever they travel, and this is not the type of joke we intend to glorify here.

Jokes, in the past, were considered for what they really are: incredibly dangerous political weapons.

The court's jester was employed by the king, and was free to say whatever he wanted, but unfree to say it to anyone but the king. The jester's speech was free because the jester was, as a political subject, unfree; his serfdom to the monarch could, depending on one's angle, be regarded as imprisonment or safe haven.[42]

At the annual White House Correspondents' Dinner it is customary for the US President to perform an act of self-parody in front of a laughing and applauding press corps—the same journalists who are supposed to hold him to account. The Dinner reveals how absorbing parody into power neutralises critics and renders authority intangible. The civil rights journalist Glenn Greenwald describes it as "the purest expression of the total blending of political power, media subservience, and vapid celebrity in one toxic, repulsive, and destructive package."[43] Just like capitalism's capacity to co-opt its critics, the adoption of humour by power renders it less vulnerable to scrutiny. The smartest is the king who, indeed, is his own jester.

The joke is the highest form of power. Activists have the action and they live the life. Theorists have the words and they know their stuff. But the joke unites both perspectives. Jokes, when politically effective, perform what everybody knew but couldn't say. The Arab Spring has seen memes which did nothing more than exposing how the system works—such as the YouTube video, *Tunisie: Qui utilise l'avion de la présidence de la République?* created by the award-winning activist blog Nawaat. The video documents, with the aid of plane-spotting pictures and the Google Earth interface, the Tunisian presidential plane on its ongoing European tour, or, more accurately, the president's wife's shopping spree with taxpayers' money.[44]

The Ben Ali story is told with inescapable effect. The crucial element is the video's accompanying music, which gives it memetic grandeur. Indeed, its chilling score of pseudo-Wagnerian bombast is both keeping the viewer glued to the screen, while parodying, and thus ridiculing, the baseless fanfare of power. Meanwhile, in Google Earth, Tunisia's presidential plane hops between Geneva's Cornavin airport, Milan Malpensa and Paris Orly in a corrupted fashion frenzy.

MEMES AND JOKES AS POLITICAL TOOLS

The meme has escaped the confines of internet forums, and is becoming a tool useful to targeted political struggles. This is illustrated by a series of interviews and essays published over the course of 2011 by the London-based ultra-left think tank, Deterritorial Support Group (DSG), which examined the meme in the wake of the emergence of Anonymous as a geopolitical force of influence. In an interview with *Dazed*, DSG asserted:

Within the past few years, memes have started to take on a totally different function, and what would have been perceived as a slightly pathetic bunch of bastards in the past are today global players in undermining international relations—namely in the complex interaction of WikiLeaks with Anonymous, 4chan and other online hooligans. There's no coherent analysis to be had of this at the moment. However 'lulz' also demonstrate their potential as part of a policy of radical refusal to the demands of capital. When asked by liberals 'Do you condone or condemn the violence of the Black Bloc?' we can only reply in unison 'This cat is pushing a watermelon out of a lake. Your premise is invalid.'[45]

Responding to a sensical question with a meaningless answer is an effective tool to negate the politics of the frame in which the question was posed; and politics has become so dispiriting and tiring that it inspires a dadaist troll mentality. The question, "do you condone or condemn," is a trap, a *gotcha*, intended to force all opposition to accord to a neoliberal frame—in other words, it is an exercise in sense-making. The absurd response refuses to participate in this exercise. It removes itself from the frame.

JOKES

The political theorist Aaron Peters, presenter of ResonanceFM's epochal *Novara* radio show, contends that jokes are one among a series of political instruments, and should be used in concert with them. Says Peters:

> The joke as a disruption of the symbolic order is useful in taking on the antagonist not through a formal and recognisable disagreement in *content* but instead as an attempt to negate the *form* of legitimate rational debate as they might have otherwise naturally presumed.
>
> Central to political contention, from protests to riots is disruption. Disruption of the circulation of goods and services during an industrial strike, a disruption of the reproduction of space with an occupation, a disruption to all social relations (or at least many of them) with the riot or insurrection. The joke, as one manifestation of the disruption of symbolic order can be seen in a similar vein in that it disrupts the circulation of discourse and is not *meant* to happen at the level of form when one engages in 'politics'. One sees this in jokes on placards at protests or stupid costumes — when protests aim at this alone they appear impotent and a meek attempt at 'subversion'

which is ultimately bereft of power. This itself might be understood as the symbolic disruption of order as opposed to the disruption of the symbolic order, a key difference between spectacle and antagonis.

However when combined with other protest repertoires, the occupation, the strike and the riot such 'jokes' become disconcerting for decision-makers. For instance amid the fires, darkness and violence in Parliament Square (from both police and protestors) on December 9th, 2010 (the apex of the UK student movement), the only visible speech acts were frequently jokes, such as 'comedy' placards. It is this mixture of the disruption of the symbolic order at a number of levels, both the physical and the communicative that disconcerts the powerful the most. When one has physical disruption but maintains a communicative order with demands then such disruption is still capable of mediation. However—when done at both the level of the symbolic and the physical the powerful inevitably ask, *what do these people want?*' One can not surmount counter-claims through 'debating' in content, instead, negation of the form and structure through which they seek to

extend their identities and reproduce
themselves as agents should be seen
as imperative.[46]

DESIGN

The first internet memes, unsurprisingly, had never even heard of "graphic design." Memes live by echo and imitation. They refute the dogma that everyone is creative. A hidden truth can become obvious overnight if it is amplified by the internet, just like the Marshall amplifier once made rock music revolutionary by making it very loud.

The aesthetic of "image macros" is a byproduct of the omnipresence of Microsoft Windows. Such images often use the font Impact, one of eleven "core fonts of the web" distributed with the operating system from 1996 to 2002. Impact (itself based on Helvetica Inserat "display" type) is a standard, wind tunnel and time-tested. The remaining Darwinian core is a bare bones typeface which can't be be reduced any further. Somehow such standards, like memes, are the survivors of a ruthlessly subtractive process. The art is in surfing the waves of reduction while not giving up on the idea. Then, even the minimal design that was ever involved has been rapidly made unnecessary as memes become online templates; when a popular meme arises, such as "condescending Wonka"[47] or "Business Cat,"[48] meme repositories such as Quickmeme and Knowyourmeme provide online template files so that anyone can make their own. Such templates then also solidify and conserve the meme aesthetic into its Microsoft-inspired "Impact" stage.

CAN JOKES BRING DOWN GOVERNMENTS?

From the perspective of graphic design, this trajectory was unanticipated and untheorized. It is unavoidable that the political design strategies emerging today make use of completely different repositories of "public" information than previous ones, and are perpetuating in trial and error rather than in the certainties of bygone era graphic design museum pieces. "Political graphic design", as a genre, has been dying for decades. As a terminally ill patient, it was supposed to be maintained by designers feeling socially, politically and environmentally "responsible." Political graphic design was then supposed to operate like a charity for universal, nonpolitical goods—effectively adding a few socially responsible footnotes to an already written-out, market-based, capitalist realist storyline. The ideologies of social design and sustainability have taken no issue with corrupted rule in formally democratic countries; they have instead presupposed, in the ideological void of the post-political, that these systems were inherently okay and just needed correction on some unethical details. Yet, the very notion that "responsibility" is the continuation of a political tradition is itself a mistake.

Rest assured that the historical picture of graphic design as a discipline inhabited by socially concerned humanists fighting for a better world is a gross misrepresentation of what this discipline has ever had to offer. It has been 99% bland (thus boring) "normality" based simply on the predict-ability of getting reasonable financial returns from running a graphic design practice. Everything else is an exception. Design historians, in search of a useful dialectic, have fed the public (or, the small partition of it that has even heard of graphic design) with the historical comparison (and thus, the false choice) between a "functionalist" approach and an opposed, "radical" one. The Dutch designers Wim Crouwel and Jan van Toorn are known as the "polar opposites" representing both these directions, which are spoonfed to every graphic design student. Both designers however, as Michael Rock has noted, merely occupied sides of the same coin.[49] Even the supposedly radical position was tied to institutions which already advocated what the designer then amplified. Both designers fostered long-established partnerships with museums and public institutions like the Postal Service. Some of the formal obses-sions of Crouwel, the systematic problem-solver whose Total Design was The Netherlands' first corporate design agency, its high modernism at the time criticised as "the new ugliness," now seem dated. Equally, some of the political complexities addressed sideways by Van Toorn, a highly talented organiser of absurd socio-political photo montages with disruptive typography, are now forgotten. Van Toorn's self-declared zenith of political activism, his "Drees stamp" for the Dutch postal service, devoted to the depiction of a former Dutch prime minister, positions the political figurehead cut-out and diagonally superimposed in an attempt to commemorate the man as an anti-icon of himself. What remains of this faux-juxtaposition is that a public institution like the Postal Service, as a platform for graphic design, could indeed give rise to radically different "solutions" to very similar "problems." This has, in graphic design, been mistaken for a permanent condition, so that extremely long periods of difference and exception to it came to seem like unwelcome deviations from a pre-established normative frame; Van Toorn himself attested to this point of view when he observed that "the discipline has abandoned the previous mental space in which it reflected on its social role."[50] Even if this were to be true, it is stunning how Van Toorn seems to disregard the crucially important role played by institutions (and organisations) and indeed attributes almost everything to the deteriorating intent of design itself. We are beginning to see now that it may have been different all along.

Rick Poynor notes that Van Toorn, while in his mid-30s with a family, did not take part in any of the 1960s protests in Amsterdam; "nor did he belong to, or work for, any radical political group, either then or later."[51] Classical "political graphic design" is exemplified by designers such as the French collective Grapus—a group of graphic artists who came together after May 1968. In their initial years Grapus' clientele consisted of trade unions and political organisations, while it later came to consist mainly of museums and cultural and charitable organisations. Grapus' work is widely praised; its co-founder Pierre Bernard was individually awarded the 2006 Erasmus Prize for the group's achievements—itself a mockery of the original politics of collective practice. Graphic design as a trade and as a client-based practice indeed may be too tied to institutional practice of any kind to constitute a revolutionary act on its own merits. The artist Thomas Hirschhorn, in an interview with Alison Gingeras, expressed such concerns when he reflected on his initial enthusiasm for radical design:

> I came to Paris to work for the graphic art collective Grapus right after school. I wanted to work for them because I admired their form and their political engagement. For me, these two elements are inseparable. (...) Yet, while working at Grapus, I began to realise that they functioned like any other commercial advertising agency. They worked for the unions (*les syndicats*), for the Communist Party... but this realisation was a shock to me. There was nothing revolutionary about this work![52]

CAN JOKES BRING DOWN GOVERNMENTS?

Grapus used the poster as an affordable and effective means of distributing a message and broadcasting it onto the streets. Effective does not mean straightforward; much of Grapus' work was dashingly complex. Pierre Bernard had "discovered the image as the vehicle of social criticism and utopian desire."[53] On a similar middle ground between criticism and utopianism rested Van Toorn's "dialogic image," which mashed multiple, conflicting messages into a collage, or montage—often serving the publicity of museums, exhibitions, and arts journals. The dialogic image permitted the viewer to draw his own conclusions, but urged them to be uneasy ones. Van Toorn and Grapus alike did their thing on a middle ground of public and state—in between collective symbols of public life and public good. Another territory of that middle ground was taken up by a design which serviced the smooth functioning of the public facilities—transport, energy, timetables, signage, the mail, and so on. The infrastructure of public institutions created a space where two different attitudes and approaches—the political-provocative, and the techno-institutional, co-existed as sides of the same coin, like they did in the art schools where such respective design attitudes were taught. During and after the privatisations of the 1980s and 1990s, the middle ground of these public institutions continued to wither and disperse into a capitalist realist, pseudo-competitive world.

What is left of political graphic design is a bit of a joke. In truth, there hasn't been a project—either as criticism or as utopia—to take its place, as the space where it used to appear has been eclipsed by a flurry of arts institutions, galleries and small presses, indeed, a hipster remainder of the taxpayer-enabled cultural middle ground.

With regard to its implications for the meme, DSG made important suggestions. In their essay, *Goatse as Industrial Sabotage*, the group suggests that the Goatse (an extremely unpleasant image of a man stretching his rectum) is in reality a return of Jan van Toorn's "dialogic image." Goatse emerged in the same way as the Rickroll did; an unsuspecting user would click on a promising link and then get "surprised." In turn then, Van Toorn's work would be a pre-interactive form of "linkbaiting"; in the absence of links to click on, the designer already combined different target images into a single collage. Was Van Toorn indeed Rickrolling his audience, *avant la lettre*? In a dialogic image, says DSG, "the design presents multiple conflicting messages, with a view to forcing a demystified, critical reading from its audience. Here it is used in a positive form, influenced by Enzensberger's theory of 'emancipatory media'; it is considered, logical, a conscious and explicit criticality, aimed at heightening a social awareness of the constructed nature of the visual environment. A criticality negotiated between an autonomous, individual designer, an adventurous client, and a broad, undifferentiated public audience—a product of a social settlement already dead in the UK, now finally being destroyed in the Netherlands."[54]

If the eclipse of the underpinning social settlement ends the effectiveness of the visual strategy, it is useful to consider what is the current "settlement." Graphic design is now a nameless collective of survivors of the (self-) destruction of paid labor. The unpaid labor of meme making, pranking and trolling, is for DSG a hitherto untapped resource in a networked type of design power, embodied by the "in-joke"—a cloaked type of worker solidarity. The dialogic image was still a relative luxury enjoyed under social democracy. In the neoliberal gulag of precarity, such amenities are cancelled out. Indeed,

[in] this scenario, the dialogic image must be reduced to a short-hand: Goatse, the in-joke, provides that. Within Goatse, the dialogic image is covert; unable to exercise any significant level of authorial control within the design process, the designer forces the critical dissonance by tapping into the in-joke. Rather than an open dialogue between worker and employer, it has become a secretive conflict; rather than a critical design image being a conscious attempt

70

to demystify design as a mediated process, it becomes an attempt to undermine and destroy the design process. Adopting the supposedly most efficient working process for capital has pushed design to eat itself.[55]

The dialogic image survives in an encapsulated form: the meme. If true, graphic design, or whatever is left of it, can now conquer information space by self-replication. In DSG's take on the Goatse, it appears that a proletariat of information workers "smuggles" the in-joke, in a concealed or abstracted form, into the space of mainstream media. This amounts to a dialogic image, but equally to something called "subliminal messaging."[56] Subliminal messaging was a phenomenon mostly seen in post-war American advertising; a message promoting alcohol or cigarettes, for example, would optically stimulate even deeper desires in the viewer that could not be addressed explicitly. The sculpted play of ice cubes submerged in a backlit whisky glass would, on closer inspection, spell out the word "sex"—promising a 007-like world of lust.[57] The portrait of a woman, when turned 180 degrees, would have her neck and arm become her legs, while her hand—touching her neck—would suddenly touch her genitals. The optical tricks of subliminal messaging are somewhat reminiscent of graphic artist M.C. Escher's work—whose paradoxes of pattern and perspective were hiding in plain sight on the printed page, and were of deep inspiration to Douglas Hofstadter in his appreciation of Dawkins' memes proposal.

Memes and lulz emerge in an age of disenchantment with political institutions. The public intellectual has also seen better days. Lulz and Lolcats bypass the "objective" mediation of information as promoted by modernist design heroes like Otl Aicher, Massimo Vignelli and Wim Crouwel—the latter's "self-image as a designer revolved around the elimination of anything inessential."[58] Indeed, internet memes don't do any mediation at all, and are all about the *inessential* taking some kind of center-stage. Memes also ignore the "subjective" approach in design, personified by Van Toorn and others. In subjective graphic design, the designer clearly identifies his or her position as a biased narrator, aiming to make the viewer aware, time and again, that the information presented has been edited and staged, and can't be qualified objectively. In a networked-image politics of "mass self-communication," these authorial gatekeeper positions are much harder to maintain; there are too many rival memes around. Memes ignore that a sender's identity would matter at all, taking no personal account for any position, claiming instead the universal, collective category of the "anonymous." But even memes can't ignore the paradigm of functionality. Paul Mason contends that "memes are a rough and ready democracy—that is, something works if you see it working."[59]

As memes transform, DSG asserts that there is still a sense of order in the chaos, as "only the minimum trace of the original joke needs to remain—or no trace at all, as long as those in on the joke can trace back the heritage of the joke to the original." [60]

NOT JUST JOKING: THE NEW
MEMETIC FRONTLINE

A most effective integration of jokes into politics can be seen at work in the Italian comedian Beppe Grillo's Five Star movement, which continues to shake up the country, landing it 25.5 percent of the votes out of nowhere in the February, 2013 elections. Grillo has used open ridicule of Italy's political system (including Monti's technocratic austerity rule) as an opening gambit for what he announces will be a fundamental recalibration of government-at-large. Says Grillo, "we cannot keep delegating politics to others. We have to do it collectively, as citizens are the ones who know their country and its problems."[61] The movement's "V-day," first organized in 2007 and now attracting many hundreds of thousands of people, weaves together the Roman figure five, Grillo's slogan *Vaffanculo* and the Guy Fawkes-inspired *V for Vendetta* meme. After his election victory, Western news outlets glossed over Grillo's political significance to instead discuss his detrimental impact on the financial markets.[62] Indeed, Grillo promises his many voters the equivalent of an end to capitalist realism.

As opposed to "reasonable debate", jokes are political weapons which deny an opponent control over the terms of the exchange by ignoring those terms entirely. Jokes are a protocol weapon of democracy, unsettling the *structure* of the encounter between oppressor and oppressed. Jokes can unsettle the "terms of service" to which political exchange is bound by its ruling ideology.

"Lulz" are useful when a political opponent is deemed unworthy to negotiate with or is loathed deeply. The Cairo-based journalist Lina Attalah says that in Egypt, jokes have become "bolder" since the fall of Mubarak. They are not an act of desperation, but of *nonchalance*—such as dancing the Harlem Shake, itself a meme, in front of the presidential headquarters.[63] The discourse of the State, Attalah explains, is fixated on the state-citizen binary. The people are completely outside of that scope. Primarily, jokes are a means to share such political insights without "analysis" being made or "opinion" being formed. "Jokes," says Attalah, "are faster than anything else."[64]

Design, having engaged the joke, operates at that speed: the fastest. It no longer traverses the "public domain" as the mediator of an institution;

instead, it is a message to and from an open-ended in-crowd. Design-as-meme is a focal point for tacit ideological coordination, a public in-joke, a general strike of common sense-making. By virtue of their ideas and actions, combined with their degree of social proximity to the well-connected nodes of the graph, designers can come to satisfy a movement's permanent hunger for new tools, pictures, and messages. What the new memetic frontline does not need, however, is a single logo, designed by some centrally appointed actor. Such was the 2011 *New York Times* ideas competition for a logo for Occupy Wall Street, initiated by designer Seymour Chwast under the erroneous title "Every Movement Needs A Logo." Some of the firms invited by Chwast were themselves designers for the Wall Street financial elite, attesting to the crippling hypocrisy of a discipline which has outsourced its ethical faculties to Icograda congresses and world peace posters printed in an edition of 1.[65] In a recent interview, one of the invited firms, Chermayeff & Geismar — who designed Chase Manhattan's corporate identity — declared that it is none of their business to evaluate the ethics of their clients' practices: "We do not feel responsible for the character of those we work for."[66] It was Chwast's own Push Pin Studios that in the 1970s designed the I HEART NY logo. This trademark has become historically linked to a "total reorientation of the city toward real estate, insurance, and finance."[67] Chwast is thus, in a typical twist of graphic design fate, intimately connected to the very roots of the problems he tries to alleviate by commissioning Occupy logos from real estate-owning Manhattan design celebrities. Inadvertently, Chwast demonstrated design's *completely failed entitlement* to represent anything other than itself. With a simple "Can I haz," any cute kitten would refute the campaign.

Another graphic design mistake was Shepard Fairey's "Occupy Hope" poster. "Mister President, we HOPE you're on our side," begs a *V for Vendetta* Guy Fawkes/Anonymous mask-wearing protester who slightly turns his head, a "dangerous" anarchist begging to be liked.[68] The message is directed at US President Barack Obama, while it follows the same visual pattern and structure as the "HOPE" poster which Fairey created in 2008 as an uncommissioned endorsement of the Obama campaign. Furthermore, this poster suggests that the person hiding behind the Anonymous mask may be Obama himself, in secret agreement with Occupy.No social movement should let itself be designed by the superstructure it revolts against; but then there are other ways in which it still gets structured and signified. Designers, rather than directly designing the messages themselves, may also create the *formats* to best channel them. Design, here, is the expression of a means to scale and involve what others do by a set of instructions. The "99%" Tumblr page features hundreds of photographs of ordinary people, telling their stories of student debt, precarity, and lack of access to health care, hand written on a sheet of paper, leaving enough space to see fragments of their faces, bodies, hands, and even bits of their houses.[69] The blog has clear directions for photography—controlled enough for the submissions to be similarly structured (for example, it was detailed that all texts should be handwritten), yet loose enough for each contributor to feel they can tell their own story with them, so that such a format or standard allows its users to no longer think about design at all.

Occupy Wall Street was, in its early stages, coordinated via Pastebin, an online text tool existing since 2002, designed to post snippets of code among computer programmers.[70] Rather than specifically being catered to or designed for protest, Pastebin was *appropriated* for that goal—it became "the ultimate hacker hangout."[71] It became a parking spot for revolutionary content: from code, to press release, to leaked data. Indeed, former Federal agent Fred Baclagan's admission to being Rickrolled was—against his will—published on Pastebin. Designers may sometimes be creating such tools and spaces: not so much designing their content, as making room for others to invent a new use, a new message, a new meaning within. It is 4chan, all over again.

AFTERWORD

MARCH, 2013

A hesitant Spring with sunshine and snow. I love this old record store, where the last remaining vinyl copy of Rick Astley's Never Gonna Give You Up was just sold. "Ungovernability" is trending on Twitter. Italy is now without a government. The Dutch government has announced another four billion euros of cuts to meet its deficit criteria; bound to capitalist realism, its coalition of liberal-conservative and social-democrat managers is fast heading for the cliffs. In Greece, the Golden Dawn, a neo-nazi political party with a paramilitary wing and strong ties to the police force, hands out food and beats up immigrants. In Portugal and Spain, millions are protesting the troika's concerted raid on democracy. The troika includes the International Monetary Fund (IMF), whose former chief, Dominique Strauss-Kahn, stood accused of sexually assaulting a cleaning lady in a New York hotel, and allegedly co-organised and participated in sex orgies which make Berlusconi's bunga bunga parties pale into insignificance. Last month, the Argentine legal philosopher Marcela Iacub published a book about her relationship with Strauss-Kahn, which she orchestrated in 2012 in order to investigate his personality. In it, she calls the former IMF chief a "half man, half pig." Strauss-Kahn complained about the "behaviour of a woman who seduces to write a book, claiming to have amorous feelings to exploit them financially," and tried to gag the author for libel. He lost. Le Nouvel Observateur *defended Iacub's writing as "a work of 'stupefying literary power' in the tradition of 'bestial' works such as Kafka's The Metamorphosis."*[72]

In the metaphor she chose for the former IMF leader, Iacub has taken a crucial next step in the ridicule of power. Hers is a step which can be defended on its artistic merit—and at the same time, she is going medieval on Strauss-Kahn, a level of scrutiny so fundamental that no one is excluded from the in-joke.

Twitter distracts me. The Eurozone troika has just bailed out Cyprus. The Cyprus austerity package, as announced by Dutch "social democrat" Jeroen Dijsselbloem, includes a seizure of up to 10% of the money in all Cypriot savings accounts—whether you are a Russian oligarch or a small-time pensioner, the troika shows no mercy. Obviously, a bank run has already started, and there is panic among the Cypriots. The troika refuses to guarantee that a similar measure—already compared to "theft"—will not be implemented in other Eurozone countries. As Forbes *writer Karl Whelan dryly comments: "Over the longer-term, I doubt if financial stability in the euro area (and the continued existence of the euro) is compatible with a policy framework that doesn't protect the savings of ordinary depositors."*[73] *Even* The Economist *calls the move "unfair, short-sighted and self-defeating."*[74]

What power will counter the austerity elites? Since they give no limits to themselves, it is all about launching rival memes. The troika already has the power of the sword—that is, the police and military protecting the buildings where politicians and the delegates gather to take all the decisions which no one wants. The troika, like the Spanish Inquisition, roams Europe and its decisions are each and every time protected, fortified, by the coercive power of the State. How much of such systemic violence can people endure before they go crazy? Indeed, Europe's techno-financial political infrastructure is its own Hosni Mubarak.

Carl Von Clausewitz famously said that war is a continuation of politics by other means. The austerity elites are indeed waging existential warfare on Europe, using an extra-political space which only they and other technocrats understand; a space where no citizen can find redress, unless they jump out of the frame once and for good. Beppe Grillo did it in Italy. Jón Gnarr did it in Iceland.

Designers and non-designers (that means everyone), now is the time for jokes. A time for ridicule and laughter and protest and screaming and general strikes. A time to publicise, on a gut level, what we feel about those in power; a time to show them our deepest, cat-like instincts. Our messages will be seen, shared and remembered. Loathe the austerity elites, deface and unmask the technocratic superstructure's lifeless avatars. Spraypaint, overload, bombard, name and shame austerity's guilty overlords with jokes that pass through each and every riot shield.

Jokes are a continuation of politics by other memes.

END NOTES

1   Andrew Higgins, "Iceland, Fervent Prosecutor of Bankers, Sees
     Meagre Returns", *New York Times*, February 3, 2012, www.
     nytimes.com/2013/02/03/world/europe/iceland-prosecutor-
     of-bankers-sees-meager-returns.html?emc=eta1&_r=0

2   Tyler Durden, "Head Of Greek Debt Office Replaced By
     Former Goldman Investment Banker", *Zero Hedge*, February
     19, 2010, www.zerohedge.com/article/head-greek-debt-office-
     replaced-former-goldman-investment-banker

3   David Milliken and Randall Palmer, "Canada's Carney named
     as Bank of England chief", *Reuters*, November 26, 2012.
     www.uk.reuters.com/article/2012/11/26/uk-britain-boe-
     idUKBRE8AP0IT20121126

4   Mark Fisher, *Capitalist Realism* (London: Zero Books,
     2009), 2.

5   David Graeber, *Debt: the First 5000 Years*, (New York: Melville
     House, 2011), 382.

6   For more on the Third Way see our essay "10 Notes on
     Speculative Design," in Giorgio Camuffo and Maddalena
     Dalla Mura (eds.), *Graphic Design Worlds*, (Milan: Mondadori
     Electa, 2011), 257-271.

7   Fisher 2009, 81.

8   Paul Mason, *Why It's Kicking Off Everywhere. The New Global
     Revolutions.* (London: Verso, 2012), 43.

9   "4chan Faq 'Who is Anonymous?'", accessed March 20, 2013,
     www.4chan.org/faq#anonymous

10   See Parmy Olson, *We Are Anonymous. Inside the Hacker
     World of LulzSec, Anonymous, and the Global Cyber
     Insurgency*, (New York: Little, Brown and Company,
     2012), 82.

11   Gabriella Coleman, "Anonymous: From the Lulz to Collective
     Action," *The New Everyday*, April 6, 2011,
     www.mediacommons.futureofthebook.org/tne/pieces/
     anonymous-lulz-collective-action

12   Original English translation of The Invisible Committee,
     The Coming Insurrection, accessed March 20, 2013,
     www.mediafire.com/?ztoijwzmzd2

13   The Invisible Committee, *The Coming Insurrection*,
     (Los Angeles: Semiotext(e), 2009).

14   Jay Babcock, "Report on 'The Coming Insurrection' book

launch at NYC Barnes and Nobles, Sephora, Starbucks", *Arthurmag*, June 15, 2009, www.arthurmag.com/2009/06/15/report-on-the-coming-insurrection-book-launch-at-nyc-barnes-and-nobles-sephora-starbucks/

15   The Invisible Committee 2009, 111-112.

16   Mason 2012, 150-51.

17   Ibid.

18   Richard Dawkins, *The Selfish Gene*, (Oxford: Oxford University Press, 1976), 192.

19   "Epimenides was a Cretan who made one immortal statement: 'All Cretans are liars.' A sharper version of the statement is simply 'I am lying'; or, 'This statement is false'. It is that last version which I will usually mean when I speak of the Epimenides paradox. It is a statement which rudely violates the usually assumed dichotomy of statements into true and false, because if you tentatively think it is true, then it immediately backfires on you and makes you think it is false. But once you've decided it is false, a similar backfiring returns you to the idea that it must be true." From Douglas R. Hofstadter, *Gödel, Escher, Bach: an eternal golden braid*, (New York: Basic Books, 1979).

20   Jeremy Trevelyan Burman, "The misunderstanding of memes: Biography of an unscientific object, 1976–1999," *Perspectives on Science* 2012, vol. 20, no. 1, Boston: The MIT Press, 86-87.

21   Ibid.

22   downtownbingosaga, "One Does Not Simply Walk into Mordor — The Origin Of Memes", *Youtube*, www.youtube.com/watch?v=r21CMDyPuGo

23   Susan Stewart, *Nonsense. Aspects of Intertextuality in Folklore and Literature*. (Baltimore and London: the John Hopkins University Press, 1980), 6.

24   MaxFarquar, "Ed Miliband These Strikes Are Wrong", *Youtube*, www.youtube.com/watch?v=PZtVm8wtyFI

25   Mark Fisher, "Reality Management: Hack-gate, Hari, Milibot and the Cyber War," *Open Democracy*, July 8, 2011, www.opendemocracy.net/ourkingdom/k-punk/reality-management-hack-gate-hari-milibot-and-cyber-war

26   Stewart 1980, 13.

27   Stewart 1980, 28-29.

28 See Antisec, "Fuck FBI Friday," November 18, 2011: www.
    pastebin.com/NwN8ehFW

29 *The Guardian* describes the transformation of the Rickroll
    from a simple prank into a resistance strategy as follows:
    "It's called the 'rick-roll'. You're innocently browsing an
    apparently useful website and see a link to something else
    that might be of interest, but when you click through to
    that destination you instead find yourself confronted with
    Astley's boyish smile, his manly croon, his awkward 1987
    dance-moves.
    The link was a fake, a trap, a dummy with the nefarious
    purpose of... bringing you face-to-face with the ridiculous.
    As with so many stupid internet fads, the rick-roll trend had
    its start at 4chan, a message-board whose lunatic, juvenile
    community is at once brilliant, ridiculous and alarming.
    4chan users had taken to 'duck-rolling' each other — tricking
    one-another into viewing a video of a, er, duck with wheels.
    In the spring of 2007 some enterprising prodigy branched off
    from this into the rick-roll. And the rest is history." "Of late,
    however, rick-rolling has begun to permeate the mainstream.
    It comes mostly courtesy of Anonymous, a diffuse group of
    hackers and activists who have declared war on the Church
    of Scientology in an initiative called Project Chanology.
    Organised without official leaders or hierarchy, Project
    Chanology manifests itself in Denial Of Service attacks
    against Scientologist websites, stupid YouTube videos,
    and in-person protests at Scientologist centres worldwide."
    See www.guardian.co.uk/music/2008/mar/19/news

30 Computer geek jargon for "the physical world."

31 See David Singh Grewal, *Network Power. The Social
    Dynamics of Globalization.* (New Haven/London: Yale
    University Press, 2008), 61.

32 Jimmy Cauty, Bill Drummond, *The Manual. How To
    Have A Number One The Easy Way.* (London: Ellipsis, 1998
    [1990]), 67.

33 Ibid, 67-68.

34 "Lolcat", *Wikipedia*, www.en.wikipedia.org/wiki/Lolcat

35 Gruppen, *Kittens #3*, www.gegen-kapital-und-nation.org/
    sites/default/files/kittens-03-web.pdf

36   Gideon Lewis Kraus, "I'm in ur internets, kontrolin ur mindz." *Wired*, September 2012, 131.

37   Ibid, 156.

38   Ethan Zuckerman, "The Cute Cat Theory Talk at Etech", www. ethanzuckerman.com/blog/2008/03/08/the-cute-cat-theory-talk-at-etech/

39   See Project Mayhem, accessed February 25, 2012, www.scribd.com/doc/80286138/Project-Mayhem-2012-12-21-2012-11-11-Imagine-We-Leak-It-ALL-DHS-National-Cyber-Security-and-Communications-Integration-Center-Bulletin-Warns-Agai

40   Jimmy Cauty, Bill Drummond 1990, 55.

41   Issandr El Amrani, "Three Decades of a Joke That Just Won't Die," *Foreign Policy*, January/February 2011, www. foreignpolicy.com/articles/2011/01/02/three_decades_of_a_joke_that_just_wont_die

42   See "Fooling Around the World: The History of the Jester; An excerpt from *Fools Are Everywhere—The Court Jester Around the World*", www.press.uchicago.edu/Misc/Chicago/640914. html

43   See Glenn Greenwald. "Dog-training the press corps." *Salon. com*, April 30, 2012, www.salon.com/2012/04/30/dog_training_the_press_corps/

44   Nawaat, "Tunisie : Qui utilise l'avion de la présidence de la République?", *Youtube*, www.youtube.com/watch?v=XRW2BJOewcc

45   Huw Nesbitt, "We Will Fight, We Will Kiss", *Dazed Digital*, www.dazeddigital.com/artsandculture/article/10260/1/deterritorial-support-group

46   Aaron Peters, e-mail interview with author, March 23, 2012.

47   "Condescending Wonka", *Quickmeme*, www.quickmeme.com/Condescending-Wonka/

48   "Business Cat", *Know Your Meme*, www.knowyourmeme.com/memes/business-cat

49   See Michael Rock, *Mad Dutch Disease*, 2013 [2003], www.2x4.org/ideas/19/Mad+Dutch+Disease+/

50   Rick Poynor, *Jan Van Toorn: Critical Practice*, (Rotterdam: 010 Publishers, 2008), 125.

51   Ibid, 85.

52   Thomas Hirschhorn interviewed by Alison Gingeras, quoted
      in "Freedom is the possibility to determine one's own conflict,
      interview with Jonas Staal by Daniel van der Velden,"
      November 28, 2006, www.jonasstaal.nl/geschreven%20werk/
      metahaven_jonasstaal.pdf

53   Hugues Boekraad, "Visual rhetoric and ethics: Pierre Bernard,
      designer for the public domain," in Hugues Boekraad, *My
      work is not my work. Pierre Bernard. Design for the public
      domain,* (Baden: Lars Müller Publishers, 2007), 37.

54   Deterritorial Support Group (DSG), *Goatse as Industrial
      Sabotage,* 2011, www.deterritorialsupportgroup.wordpress.
      com/2011/09/27/goatse-as-industrial-sabotage/

55   Ibid.

56   In this matrix, a sexually stimulating element would be
      hidden inside an otherwise conventional-looking visual
      message. Such subliminal advertisements harboured a secret
      dialogue between their official content and suppressed,
      hidden content, but not as an expression of worker solidarity—
      the goal was to sell more products. To many of the inventors
      and worshippers of the meme, this probably wouldn't matter.
      Recent studies suggest that embedding subliminal content in
      messages does "work", especially if the content is "negative"—
      one example being a roadsign which says *Kill Your Speed*
      instead of *Slow Down.* See www.sciencedaily.com/
      releases/2009/09/090928095343.htm and www.telegraph.co.
      uk/science/science-news/6232801/Subliminal-advertising-
      really-does-work-claim-scientists.html

57   One is reminded of the famous Monty Python "wink wink,
      nudge nudge" sketch, where a man tries to enjoy "in-jokes"
      with another man about the sex act until he finally asks him
      innocently for advice: "Well, what's it like?"

58   Camiel van Winkel, *The Regime of Visibility*, (Rotterdam:
      NAi Publishers, 2005), 130.

59   Rod Stanley, "Paul Mason, Why It's All Kicking Off", *Dazed
      Digital*, www.dazeddigital.com/artsandculture/
      article/12271/1/paul-mason-why-its-all-kicking-off

60   DSG 2011.

61   See Laura Cugusi, "The Triumph of Dissidence. Italian Five
      Star Movement surprises everyone with elections results,

including itself," *Egypt Independent*, February 28, 2013.

62   See James Legge, "Beppe Grillo Suggests Italy Might Leave the Euro", *The Independent,* March 2, 2013, www.independent.co. uk/news/world/europe/beppe-grillo-suggests-italy-might-leave-the-euro-8517790.html

63   Jill Reilly, "Egyptian Protestors Harlem Shake Outside Headquarters of President Morsi", *Daily Mail*, March 1, 2013, www.dailymail.co.uk/news/article-2286476/Egyptian-protestors-Harlem-Shake-outside-headquarters-President-Morsi.html

64   Lina Attalah, conversation with author, February 28, 2013.

65   Seymour Chwast, "Every Movement Needs A Logo," *The New York Times*, October 8, 2011, www.nytimes.com/interactive/2011/10/08/opinion/20111009_OPINION_LOGOS.html

66   Aaron Kenedi, "Marks Men: An Interview With Ivan Chermayeff, Tom Geismar, and Sagi Haviv of Chermayeff & Geismar", *Imprint Magazine*, September 14, 2011, www. imprint.printmag.com/branding/marks-men-an-interview-with-ivan-chermayeff-tom-geismar-and-sagi-haviv-of-chermayeff-geismar/

67   Alex Vitale, "NYPD and OWS: A Clash of Styles," in *Occupy! Scenes from Occupied America*, (London/New York: Verso, 2011), 75.

68   Simone Wilson, "Shepard Fairey Designs 'Occupy Hope' Poster, Replaces Obama's Face With 'V for Vendetta' Mask", *LA Weekly*, November 28 2011, blogs.laweekly.com/informer/2011/11/shepard_fairey_designs_occupy.php

69   We Are The 99 Percent, *Tumblr,* www.wearethe99percent. tumblr.com/

70   "A Fluid Protest Movement Finds a Forum to Match," The New York Times, October 9, 2011, www.nytimes. com/2011/10/10/business/media/pastebin-helps-occupy-wall-street-spread-the-word.html

71   Matt Brian, "Pastebin: How a popular code-sharing site became the ultimate hacker hangout", *The Next Web*, June 5 2011, www.thenextweb.com/socialmedia/2011/06/05/pastebin-how-a-popular-code-sharing-site-became-the-ultimate-hacker-hangout/

END NOTES

72   Henry Samuels, "Dominique Strauss-Kahn: my affair with the 'king of pigs', by Marcela Iacub", *The Telegraph*, February 21, 2013, www.telegraph.co.uk/news/worldnews/europe/france/9885848/Dominique-Strauss-Kahn-my-affair-with-the-king-of-pigs-by-Marcela-Iacub.html

73   Karl Whelan, "Cyprus Depositor Tax: Genius Plan or the End of the Euro?", *Forbes Magazine*, March 16 2013, www.forbes.com/sites/karlwhelan/2013/03/16/cyprus-depositor-tax-genius-plan-or-the-end-of-the-euro/

74   Shumpeter Blog, "Unfair, short-sighted and self-defeating", *The Economist*, March 16 2013, www.economist.com/blogs/schumpeter/2013/03/cyprus-bail-out

BELYAYEVO FOREVER
PRESERVING THE GENERIC
BY KUBA SNOPEK

BEFORE AND AFTER
THE PATHOLOGY OF SPATIAL CHANGE
BY EYAL AND INES WEIZMAN

LESS IS ENOUGH
ON ARCHITECTURE AND ASCETICISM
BY PIER VITTORIO AURELI

THE DOT-COM CITY
SILICON VALLEY URBANISM
BY ALEXANDRA LANGE

SPLENDIDLY FANTASTIC
ARCHITECTURE AND POWER GAMES
IN CHINA
BY JULIA LOVELL

DARK MATTER AND TROJAN HORSES
A STRATEGIC DESIGN VOCABULARY
BY DAN HILL

MAKE IT REAL
ARCHITECTURE AS ENACTMENT
BY SAM JACOB

CAN JOKES BRING DOWN GOVERNMENTS?
MEMES, DESIGN AND POLITICS
BY METAHAVEN

ISBN 978-0-9929146-8-4

Printed and bound by Printondemand-Worldwide
Published by Strelka Press

Copyright 2013 Strelka Press
Strelka Institute for Media, Architecture & Design
www.strelkapress.com

First edition.

The typeface used within this book is called Lazurski, it was designed
at the Soviet type design bureau, Polygraphmash, by Vladimir Yefimov
in 1984. It is a homage to a 1960s font designed by Vadim Lazurski
that was inspired by Italian typefaces of the early 16th century.